EASY WAYS TO
MANAGE
DIFFICULT NEIGHBOURS

Jennie Willett

1st edition

TSL Publications

Published in Great Britain in 2019
By TSL Publications, Rickmansworth

ISBN / 978-1-912416-74-5

Jennie Willett is a free-lance lecturer, trainer, therapist and writer. As a lecturer she specialises in adult teacher education, on how people learn. She also delivers personal development and management training courses for colleges and various organisations. Her voluntary work has included working with Victim Support, taking a lead on bullying issues. She has a private practice covering all areas of personal development, stress/time management and cognitive behaviour therapy.

A life without challenge is no life at all

This book is dedicated to the memory of

Frank Kittel and Mary Daly late of Pinner Hill, London

Wonderful neighbours, wonderful friends.

Difficult neighbour relationships can be a major cause of stress. This book deals with managing the stress caused by the thoughtless behaviour of neighbours.

The aim of this book is to:

- Reduce stress.
- Teach how to set and maintain boundaries, physically and metaphorically.
- Teach assertive dialogue.
- Show methods of negotiating win/win.
- Understand causes of difficult behaviour.
- Understand and accept difficulties.
- Self-assess own responsible neighbour behaviour.
- Learn how to nip difficult behaviour in the bud.
- Understand and manage own emotions and reactions.
- Teach resilience techniques.
- Understand human nature and what motivates neighbours to act in unacceptable ways.
- Highlight the damage caused by not handling difficulties in a professional, non-emotional manner.
- Highlight the benefits of acting with integrity, however angry you feel.

There are no guarantees that the strategies will work as no two situations are the same but it is worth aiming for win/win in difficult situations and the main focus of this book is to reduce the stress caused by inconsiderate and difficult neighbour behaviour.

The book does not cover legal disputes;
it is about avoiding litigation and the expense.
If you have a legal problem firstly contact citizensadviceuk

For most of my life I have been extremely fortunate with my neighbours over many moves.
They have been amazing, exceptional people and remained friends.

There are no personal examples in this book.

CONTENTS

ACTION NOT WORRY

I am tired of reading books and articles in magazines, Internet sites where I have to trawl through pages of text to get to a list of points as to what I do NOW. So here is a list of options. You can read the rest later.

- Stop your thoughts going round and round in your mind; you will not solve anything that way.
- Never act or react in anger.
- Only deal in facts, not feelings/emotions.
- Write down what happened. Exactly what happened. No emotions, or what you think happened. Facts.
- Write down all your options for dealing with the situation. Reading this book is one.
- Try the Internet for advice.
- Forget past deeds, just deal with the present one.
- Unless it is urgent and needs immediate attention, put your notes away for 24 hours.
- Do something to distract your thoughts.
- See how you feel about the situation in 24 hours.

All of the above will put you in control.

YOUR HOME IS MORE
THAN JUST A HOME

For the purpose of dealing with difficult neighbours you need to think of your home as a business.

Do everything to protect your major investment from neighbour disputes, which will be recorded against your property. People often forget this and get into all kinds of difficulties with their neighbours that cause ongoing problems because they haven't been managed correctly in the first place. By remembering this point your home will remain your sanctuary and not become part of a battleground.

'Seek First to Understand, then be understood'

Steven Covey
7 Habits of Highly Effective People

Translated, means you need to understand what is going on with your neighbours and then you need to put your boundaries in place.

From my research, in most cases where neighbour difficulties have gone on for a long time is due to not setting boundaries (physical and metaphorical) from the beginning. People have wanted to get along with their neighbours so they have let a few small incidents go without comment or action. Then something more serious happens and the passive behaviour turns aggressive. This book sets out to avoid that happening.

People often recover and forgive/forget minor neighbour disputes and all will seem fine, maybe for a long time; then another incident occurs. Unfortunately the brain remembers very quickly the emotions felt with all the previous incidents and these can come to the fore when trying to deal with what to others seems quite innocuous. It may seem like you are overreacting but it is only the brain reminding you of previous deeds.

Cognitive Behaviour Therapy Forms are an effective way of working through these emotions until you are dealing with just the facts.

'Mind over Mood' by Greenberger and Padesky shows you how to use these forms.

(You can find CBT forms on line but you need specific forms for dealing with anxiety and emotions.)

By doing a CBT exercise you will save yourself on stress and any irreversible damage caused by reacting to emotions and not facts.

SAFETY FIRST

Your safety and that of your family and friends has to come first. Do not tackle any difficult situation which could compromise safety.

THE MOST COMMON CAUSES OF NEIGHBOUR DISPUTES

- Inconsiderate parking.
- Noise.
- Animals.
- Late night parties.
- Boundary disputes.
- Shared amenities.
- Maintaining shared amenities.
- Fences/hedges.
- Trees.
- Overgrown gardens.
- Rights of way.
- Hygiene. (including not adhering to rules about disposal of rubbish).
- Bonfires.
- Shouting/arguing/bad language.
- **Jealousy.**

There is much advice on line for these and other problems. I suggest you do as much research as possible before taking further action.

This book deals mainly with the stress caused by difficult behaviour.

What makes a good neighbour?

Would you like to take the neighbour test?

See page 18.

HOW TO USE THIS BOOK

For those of you who experience difficult relationships with your neighbours life can be miserable. Even worse, cause problems, if you own your own home, when you want to sell.

This book aims to reduce the stress caused by neighbours and prevent neighbour disputes from devaluing your property.

You will need to read through the book to find an approach that works best for you. There is no one right way to deal with difficult neighbours; it depends on personalities, background, age, health issues to name a few. If your neighbours are breaking the law then you need to consider a different action and take professional advice.

In some cases it is effective to let matters go and in others to nip the behaviour in the bud, this is where you have to make difficult decisions. This book is about creating and maintaining boundaries, literally and metaphorically. Learning how to identify types of neighbours and types of behaviour is important. When we understand behaviour and human nature in general it makes it easier for dealing with difficulties without emotion and achieving win/win.

The skills you need are:

- Tolerance.
- Integrity.
- Resilience.
- Listening skills. Listen more than you speak.
- An understanding of human nature.
- Assertiveness.
- The ability not to personalise.
- The ability not to dwell, to let go and move on.
- Being able to react to facts not emotions.

With neighbour difficulties, think of your home as a business and do everything to protect your major investment from disputes which will be recorded against your property. This is often forgotten and people get into all types of problems with their neighbours forgetting the implications. By remembering this your home will remain your sanctuary and not become part of a battleground.

Problems with stress occur when people take neighbours' bad behaviour, personally. Remember not to personalise and it will reduce stress. When people act as if they don't like you; it is usually themselves they don't like, not you. Well-adjusted people are tolerant and will behave in a dignified manner when a problem occurs, seeking a win/win result.

It is often the case that when people's lives are not going in the direction they wish and they have no control that they will start to pick on neighbours; on petty things, that is why studying human nature is useful.

Your friends are your friends. Your neighbours are neighbours first and maybe are or will become friends. But, they will always be neighbours first and protecting their property will override friendship issues. Be clear on this before becoming too friendly.

Ask yourself the question, if your neighbours were not neighbours would they be the type of people who would be your friends?

Once you are confident you are living amongst responsible, caring people then friendships may develop.

Neighbour difficulties are diverse and complex. This book offers you suggestions and choices for how you deal with any situation. The book is like a tool-box, you need to find the right tool for the job. At times some tools will not work. Nothing is guaranteed. It is trial and error.

If you maintain integrity, aim for win/win where possible and do the right thing then you have a good chance of succeeding in building good, respectful neighbour relationships.

There are laws protecting the rights of home-owners and neighbours but this book aims to, where possible, avoid the need for litigation.

NEIGHBOUR SELF ASSESSMENT

Are you a responsible neighbour?

(this is only a guide – use pencil and you can use it again)

1. Do you introduce yourself to new neighbours?
        YES/NO/SOMETIMES

2. Do you introduce yourself when you move into a new locality?
        YES/NO/SOMETIMES

3. If you share a party wall(s) with your neighbours are there any appliances which make a noise on the adjoining walls?
        YES/NO/SOMETIMES

4. If you own pets, are they kept under control so as not to disturb?   YES/NO/SOMETIMES

5. Do you observe parking etiquette?
        YES/NO/SOMETIMES

6. Is your rubbish dealt with efficiently, tidily and hygienically?
        YES/NO/SOMETIMES

7. Do you inform your neighbours of parties/gatherings?
        YES/NO/SOMETIMES

8. Do you inform neighbours of building works?
        YES/NO/SOMETIMES

9. Do you restrict the time and use of noisy garden equipment?
        YES/NO/SOMETIMES

10. Do your guests leave your property quietly late at night?
        YES/NO/SOMETIMES

11. Is your property maintained in keeping with the locality?
        YES/NO/SOMETIMES

12. Are your gardens neat and tidy?
YES/NO/SOMETIMES

13. Clear safe boundaries (fencing/hedges/walls)?
YES/NO/SOMETIMES

14. Are you friendly/helpful to your neighbours?
YES/NO/SOMETIMES

15. Would your neighbours consider you responsible?
YES/NO/SOMETIMES

16. If you are a flat dweller do you keep noise to a minimum?
YES/NO/SOMETIMES

17. Do you avoid gossip/duplicity?
YES/NO/SOMETIMES

18. Are you a nosey neighbour?
YES/NO/SOMETIMES

19. Are you able to rise above petty issues?
YES/NO/SOMETIMES

20. Are you able to forget the past and forgive neighbour behaviour?
YES/NO/SOMETIMES

21. Do you judge your neighbours without knowing them?
YES/NO/SOMETIMES

22. Would you describe yourself as a considerate neighbour?
YES/NO/SOMETIMES

23. Respect the privacy of neighbours when they are using their garden.
YES/NO/SOMETIMES

24. Do your prefer not to acknowledge/socialise with your neighbours?
YES/NO/SOMETIMES

25. Are you a tolerant neighbour?
YES/NO/SOMETIMES

What did you find out about yourself from doing this questionnaire?

If you answered 'sometimes' think about it and could you make some changes?

Is there any area you need to work on? Get other members of the family to take the test and compare results.

Writing this book has not been easy as there is no one formula. From my research I have been told so many ghastly stories of behaviour and realise dealing with difficult neighbour behaviour is not an exact science. Every case is different, therefore you have to experiment to see what brings a resolution.

Problems are made worse if you have high expectations of your neighbours, expecting them to be pleasant, friendly and responsible. Let go of any expectations to avoid disappointment and you may be surprised.

In the beginning, until you get to know your neighbours, remember not to be over friendly; remain polite, pleasant and assertive. Being assertive means not allowing them to cross your boundaries. It means being able to say 'no' to an unreasonable request without feeling guilty.

UNDERSTANDING HUMAN NATURE

Once you become a student of human nature and understand the reasons why people are difficult, it makes it much easier to respond and not react.

Try this exercise:

Write a profile of all your difficult neighbours.

Age, status, health – as much as you know.

Once you have written a profile you may find it easier not to personalise and to plan how you will approach a situation. After doing this exercise some of my students said they felt sorry for their difficult neighbour. An interesting turn-around.

The best form of revenge is to feel sorry for someone. No need to say it. Just feel it.

People who are not nice to others cannot be having a happy life.

TREAT YOUR HOME AS A BUSINESS

Whether rented or owned, it is still a business. If you rent, you want to have a record as a good tenant. If you own your home you have to ensure you have nothing negative logged against your property. This has to be foremost in your mind when dealing with any situation. It doesn't mean avoiding as that can be a huge mistake. It means thinking before you act.

When you feel you would really like to tell your neighbours what you think of them that is the time to keep your mouth firmly shut. Go for a long walk away from your property to get rid of the adrenalin.

You look after your home so it increases in value. Its value may be affected if you have now or in the past had difficulties with your neighbours.

You may have to learn to co-exist with people you would not normally choose to associate with and therefore tolerance is a big part of being a responsible neighbour.

Those who have kind, friendly, responsible neighbours are extremely fortunate.

DO YOUR RESEARCH

Even if you have found the home of your dreams, do as much research as you can before signing contracts. This applies to renting and buying. When we fall in love with a property we tend to overlook this research and live to regret it. The negative aspects will come into their own once you have moved in.

The following is recommended:

- Visit the area and property as much as you can before signing a contract.
- Visit at various times of the day and night.
- Walk around the neighbourhood, you see more on foot.
- Ask to view the property at different times of day as many vendors will ask their neighbours to keep their barking dogs quiet while viewings are taking place.
- How do you feel about children/teenagers? They have a right to enjoy their gardens; would you be affected by their noise or welcome it?
- If you are noise sensitive, make several visits and walk out into the garden each time.
- Ask questions about the neighbours, have a checklist ready. Vendors are not allowed to lie. You could ask them to sign the checklist but this must be your decision; it may put some vendors off, so be careful. It is your choice.
- Be aware of shared drives/access ways; often a major cause of problems. For these to work efficiently it is essential to be on good terms with neighbours.
- Check at evenings and weekends the parking situation.
- Check what backs onto the property.

- If the property is near churches, nurseries, schools, clubs and any other public amenities check on opening and closing times.
- Check what businesses are being run from people's homes. For example, second-hand car dealers. Cars may be hidden behind trees/hedges but these can be chopped down. More and more people are now working from home.
- Unfortunately, when selling, people can lie about neighbours and the area, so you need to do your own research.
- Look out for anything you know would annoy and spoil your peace and lifestyle.

You cannot expect to get it totally right but by doing your research beforehand you should limit any nasty surprises.

TYPES OF NEIGHBOURS

Successful people are those who understand human nature. By understanding the difficult behaviour of your neighbours it will help you to manage it.

For example, your neighbour might be lonely, doesn't get out much, they may be envious of your lifestyle. You see the reason for their behaviour. Information is power. You understand where they are coming from and now they need to understand that you are going to put boundaries in place. This also prevents you from taking behaviour personally and gives you a chance to stand back and take time before formulating your responses.

Selfish . . .

. . . This neighbour has no regard for others and will do whatever they wish.

These are some examples I have been given:

- Regular late night parties without informing neighbours, especially in the summer when parties are held in gardens with loud music.

- Noise levels all times of the day and night from DIY, without informing neighbours.

- Revving up of motor vehicles all times of the day and night.

- Smoking of illegal substances in the garden.

- Indiscriminate with litter.

Social Climber/Snob . . .

. . . Protective of keeping the neighbourhood status and may look down on those different from themselves.

Insecure people but will look after their property and be responsible neighbours.

Animal Lover . . .

This neighbour often likes animals more than people.

They will constantly feed birds and other animals thus making their property an easy target for rodents and foxes. They will see it as their right continually to feed birds, partly because they enjoy seeing the birds come to their garden, which is a valid point, however, birdseed attracts rodents. A proven point. The local council will pay a visit, however handle this carefully and consider the repercussions.

Dogs barking all times of the day and night.

Boundaries will need to be set if their behaviour affects your property. They will not see their barking dog as a problem. It's what dogs do.

However if a neighbour asks you if their barking dog is a problem, however nice the neighbour is, be honest, otherwise, saying 'no, its fine, could come back to haunt you; for example if they get a second dog.

Say *'thank you for asking, I do hear the barking.'* Tone of voice is important; calm, firm and genuine. Do not prefix with 'sorry. You may get an apology, you may not, but you have been honest.

Nosey . . .

.. . . Every neighbourhood has at least one nosey neighbour. They like to know everything that is going on. Will ask direct personal questions. May observe activities from behind their curtains. Very useful as security watch but can be intrusive and irritating.

Immediately set boundaries by not giving away any personal information. Change the subject, to the weather, completely miss the point. It is rare they will repeat the question. If they do ask again, just don't answer.

Here are some responses for dealing with nosey/intrusive questions. You will need to find those which work best for you.

Sometimes questions are direct, at other times they are heavily camouflaged: Practise tone of voice. When the questions are asked, firstly, allow silence before responding. Lower your voice. Calm, non-emotional tone. This shows confidence.

Gosh. That's a direct question.

I wouldn't dream of boring you with my personal life.

I'm interested why have asked that?

Now that's a question I'm not going to answer.

I know you will understand but I prefer not to discuss.

Good question, not sure how I'm going to answer that.

Or you can completely miss the point. I'm really well, how are you?

Noise Sensitive . . .

. . . cannot bear any noise whatsoever.

This is difficult. You need to assess whether your noise is unreasonable. Do not be too quick to acquiesce to their requests or you may find this situation escalates. At the same time, don't overreact, be defensive or take it personally.

Some ideas for responses:

'*I will monitor this now you have mentioned it.*' (this shows you have taken their request seriously but you haven't committed yourself to anything.)

'*Have I understood this correctly you are saying . . .*'

You may not have to say anything more, just your tone of voice will show you have understood.

I appreciate you are sensitive to noise but my children are just doing what children do and I am careful about the times they are allowed to play in the garden. However, thank you for bringing it my notice.

Over-friendly . . .

. . . Beware of the over-friendly neighbours when you first move into your property.

The over-friendly sometimes become enemies. It seems great at first, you are new and there is all this kindness and help. Remember not to get too friendly until you establish that you share the same values. Set boundaries at the very beginning. It earns respect.

This is the situation that causes the most problems.

For a lot of people their gardens are a sanctuary, they like their home and they like their privacy to be respected. They may not want to chat over the fence. A polite 'good morning' and moving on is the best practice if you wish to maintain your privacy.

From my research I heard about neighbours using a trampoline and calling and waving to other neighbours as they jumped up and down!

With neighbours who keeping knocking at your door. Remember just because someone knocks at your door, you do not have to answer it. Set the boundary early on.

Non-Mixer . . .

. . . This can be a bonus. As long as you are on speaking terms, let them keep themselves to themselves. It is their home and their right. Do not take the behaviour personally. Respect their wishes and accept.

However, do not confuse a non-mixer with someone who is shy and lonely. It is the duty of us all to look out for vulnerable, lonely neighbours. Do note that just because someone is lonely and vulnerable does not give them the right to be rude.

Do-Gooder . . .

This neighbour can be a fantastic bonus to the neighbourhood or a bit of nuisance. They support and fund raise for local charities, take an interest in all neighbourhood changes, events, crimes, planning applications etc.

If you do not wish to get involved, and that is your right, do not feel guilty or defend yourself. They will soon get the message and move on to someone else.

Bearing in mind the phrase *never defend or justify yourself, except in a court of law'* is very useful. You can ask for time to think about their request. Try not to lie because once you tell one lie, you then have to tell more and you will lose your integrity. Keep it simple, *'I'm not able to do that.'* If they should be rude enough to ask why, then repeat what you said, word for word, in a very calm voice.

The Project Neighbour . . .

. . . There are some neighbours who make it almost a project to object and not get along with their neighbours. Usually, but not always, elderly, unhappy people. By focusing on the shortcomings of their neighbours it gives them a project. Recognise this type of neighbour and accept, but don't take the behaviour personally.

By accept, that doesn't mean, you allow them to say or do anything you are not happy with. It means accept the kind of person they are. Acceptance, puts you in control. Non-acceptance and taking personally puts them in control.

The Apologetic Neighbour . . .

. . . Has a 'go' at you for something they are not happy about then apologises. This is clever. The neighbour is disrespecting your boundaries and then apologising. They feel that their apology makes everything all right.

You can be fooled into thinking that because they have apologised, everything will return to how it was. What actually happens is that they repeat the behaviour. Speak their mind, apologise and repeat.

It is a manipulative way of getting what they want. Remember to stand back and respond assertively.

- *Thank you for your apology, but I am still not happy with the situation.*

- *I accept your apology. Thank you.*

- *I accept your apology, now can we discuss a solution?*

- *I accept your apology this time but please don't speak to me like that again.*

- *It was an unpleasant situation and I note your apology.*

The Jealous Neighbour . . .

. . . is the most common cause of neighbour difficulties.

Some triggers:

- When people move into a new property they usually make immediate changes, often a complete refurbishment. Other neighbours may wish to do the same but do not have the finance or the ideas.
- Newer and better vehicles.
- Children at posh schools.
- Perceived higher social status.
- Enviable career.
- Younger.
- Smart, attractive.
- Popular.
- Happy.
- Perceived better lifestyle.

High financial bracket.

The Retired Neighbour . . .

. . . can be a bonus or a nightmare. Just because they are elderly doesn't mean they will be the perfect neighbour, or nice people. You may feel you have to tread very carefully because they have age on their side. Other neighbours may seem to side with them rather than you, the newcomer.

Again, set boundaries from the very beginning. Don't be afraid of offending or be too ready to accede to their requests; as long as you are not being unkind, difficult or a nuisance.

They may seemingly ask for innocuous things to be accepted, you agree; this is a metaphorical step in your door. The more you agree to their little requests the more difficult they will become later on. Set those boundaries early on.

'Your children are very noisy, I wonder if you could ask your children to be a little quieter in the garden.' This seems innocuous at first and easy to say 'of course.' Or, snap back. *'they are only children enjoying themselves.'* Both reactions will do nothing for future good neighbourliness.

Instead . . . use an assertive responsive.

Take a mental step back. Listen, hear all they have to say. Repeat their words back to them, in a calm, low voice.

'I don't feel my children are unduly noisy and it is difficult to ask children to be 'a little quieter' but thank you for bringing it to my attention, now please excuse me I have to go.

Be direct, be business-like.

If they try to continue say, *please forgive me, I have to go . . .*

YOUR HOME IS YOUR CASTLE

Wherever you live, be it in a one room studio, or a mansion, your home is your castle. It is your safe haven. You need to protect your safe haven.

Also, remember others have a right to their own safe haven too.

Unless you live in the middle of nowhere without immediate neighbours, you need to be considerate to your neighbours. However considerate you are is no guarantee that the consideration will be returned. By accepting this fact, you are taking a step towards reducing your stress.

People are protective of their 'castles' as you will be. They will watch, with concern, any alterations you make to your home and gardens in case it affects them.

DIPLOMACY

Always try to speak to a neighbour first before taking any further action, in the hope the situation will be resolved. Many people just don't realise they are causing a nuisance, or breaking any rules.

The best phrase, delivered in a non-confrontational manner, low tone of voice.

You may not be aware that . . .

> *. . . your guests often block my drive.*

> *. . . your children's music is keeping my baby awake.*

> *. . . your dog whines and barks a lot when you are out.*

You don't need to say anything else. You have raised the point in a non-confrontational manner. It is then up to them whether or not they take any action. In most cases, because you have been 'nice' about it they will regulate the behaviour. It is called 'nipping it in the bud.' This avoids the situation building and building and causing you more stress.

YOU DO NOT HAVE TO LIKE YOUR NEIGHBOURS IN ORDER TO LIVE HARMONIOUSLY

Take it as a bonus if you have neighbours you like.

If you don't like your neighbours you can still live harmoniously if you follow the rules of being a responsible neighbour and set your own boundaries from the beginning. It is easier to maintain boundaries set at the beginning, however, they can still be set later, but they will just be harder to maintain.

If you don't like your neighbours, or they don't like you, just get over it. It doesn't matter. We all have different values and come from diverse backgrounds. We cannot expect others to have the same values as we may have.

Many people have not been taught manners, or how to behave responsibly, therefore tolerance, whilst keeping boundaries in place, is of utmost importance.

Tolerance and acceptance reduces stress.

ALWAYS THINK 'WIN/WIN'

In whatever situation you find yourself, think 'win/win.' However angry and frustrated, plan a way where each of you benefit.

Useful phrases:

- *How can we negotiate a solution?*
- *There has to be a way round this?*
- *Let's find a way that benefits all parties.*
- *What are your ideas for win/win?*
- *How can we achieve win/win?*

Imagine using these phrases:

Noisy Party

'Thank you for letting me know you are having a party. How can we achieve win/win where you enjoy a party and we are not kept awake in the early hours?'

Feeling angry and powerless will achieve nothing.

Asking someone to intervene on your behalf is an option.

NEVER TAKE BAD BEHAVIOUR PERSONALLY

However badly your neighbour behaves, even if it is directed at you, never, ever take It personally. People behave badly for a variety of reasons:

- They don't know how to behave correctly.
- They are going through a stressful period.
- They are just unhappy.

Avoid becoming a victim by taking behaviour personally. Victims never win.

It is common that when neighbours are being difficult or down-right nasty the innocent party starts to look for reasons they may have caused the behaviour. Also, it is natural for other neighbours to see both sides because they will have listened to all the gossip. That's what other neighbours tend to do. Enjoy listening to the gossip, then retreat, even if they appear to be good friends with you. Try to avoid involving other neighbours, remembering it is human nature to enjoy a good gossip. You can seek advice/counselling from someone outside of your neighbourhood, who will be able objectively to see both sides but will ultimately be on your side to find a solution.

FORGET THE PAST . . .

Try to forget past incidents and aim to start afresh, in a positive manner.

Leave the past where it belongs, in the past. There is merit in this, depending on the behaviour. Learn from the past, what could you have done to reduce stress?

A genuine one-off misunderstanding is recoverable.

If your neighbours are displaying an unfortunate side of their character showing different values from your own then it is better not to get too friendly.

For those who have experienced constant problems with neighbours this will be extremely difficult. Start with acceptance rather than forgetting. In time the past will fade but there may be triggers in the future which will bring back past emotions. They are just emotions. If they are strong, try some cognitive behaviour therapy. You can do this with a therapist or on your own. Most CBT books contain thought processing forms. It is beneficial to learn how to use these forms. The result is you have worked through your thoughts until the emotions have reduced. It helps you focus on facts not emotions.

LISTEN MORE THAN YOU SPEAK

When a neighbour is 'having a go' at you:

- Listen, without speaking.
- If you need to speak, repeat key words/phrases.

Neighbour: *Your trees need cutting, they are blocking my light . . .'*

You: 'My trees are blocking your light?'

Wait for their response.

- Respond, don't react.
- Take a deep breath before responding:

Thank you, I will investigate/get back to you/think about what you have said . . .

If they have a genuine case, however rude they may have been, you will need to negotiate a solution. Be business-like, imagine it is a job and you are at work.

GOLDEN RULES

- When you first move in, be polite to your neighbours but not over-friendly.
- Be clear in your own mind what you want from the community. Do you want to take an active part? Or keep your privacy. You have a choice. It is your home, your life.
- Establish boundaries from the beginning. We often don't recognise the first signs. Be alert. Make sure your physical and emotional boundaries are in place and correct.
- Establish boundaries by what you will and will not accept. These are best set at the beginning, however pleasant your neighbours appear. Setting boundaries later can be difficult. For example, the moment a neighbour blocks your drive, ask politely for them to move. If you let them do it several times, you seethe inside and then driven by anger and frustration ask them to move, you will be seen to be the one at fault.
- If a neighbour is unhappy with something you are doing, think before responding. You can even play for time by saying 'I will come back to you on this.' (note it is a statement not a question). If you acquiesce too quickly, you may find their complaining becomes a habit. Start as you mean to carry on. If you are a gardener it is called 'nipping it in the bud.'
- Do apologise if you know you have done something which is not in the best interests of other neighbours. For example, a powerful bonfire, a late party.
- The minute you find yourself getting uptight about neighbour behaviour, make a plan of action. Take the stress as a warning.
- Do not discuss your neighbour difficulties with other neighbours, you may find that you get unhelpful comments:

- *Oh, I get on ok with them.*
- *What do you think you did to cause that?*
- *They're elderly, they don't get out much.*

You start to think you are at fault, even feel guilty.

- Seek a resolution as quickly as possible.
- Beware of the neighbour who invites you round for coffee, dinner, or barbecue and then after a really friendly evening, mentions something that is bothering them. You feel trapped by their hospitality. In this situation, be honest *'I feel a bit awkward about what you have just said, I'm going now and will discuss this another time.'*
- Beware of the neighbour who enquires how you are then raises an issue. If you reply, *'I haven't time to discuss this now, are you around . . . !'* Or, *'I feel a bit awkward about what you have just said . . . I don't know how to answer, must go, I will get back to you.*

This will give you back control and some thinking time.

THE TIME TO KEEP QUIET . . .

Is when you feel you must say something.

There will be times when you would like to tell difficult neighbours exactly what you think of them. DON'T. You will be labelled 'as bad as them.'

However rude the person is, remain extremely polite. Politeness and good manners are the most powerful weapons you have, don't be afraid to use them.

If you feel angry and frustrated, walk away until you have calmed down.

There will be occasions when you will need to be assertive, if the other party is getting out of control or you feel threatened:

- Lower your voice – very powerful.
- Say what you feel you have to, in a calm, measured tone.
- If you feel the situation is escalating out of control, or you feel unsafe, walk away. Or, summon help.

Know when to walk away.

AVOID DUPLICITY

If a neighbour discusses another neighbour with you, desist from joining in, however much you agree. You may feel awkward but you will benefit in the long term.

If your neighbour is discussing another with you, you can be sure they will be discussing you at some point with someone else.

Be known as someone who doesn't gossip, is not duplicitous.

THE NEIGHBOUR WHO KEEPS KNOCKING AT YOUR DOOR

If you have a policy of not opening your front door unless you are expecting someone then this neighbour will soon get the message.

Have a spy-hole so you can see who is at the front door.

You do not have to open your front door just because someone is there.

Encourage emails or texts, it gives you thinking time.

THE NEIGHBOUR WHO WAYLAYS YOU

This type of behaviour is from a neighbour who may be looking for when you leave or enter your home. They can be an extreme nuisance, especially if you are just off to work, on the school run or coming home from a busy day. Learn assertive responses. If you don't, they will take their behaviour as acceptable, become a nuisance and cause bigger problems in the long term.

- *Please forgive me, I'm in a hurry.*
- *Could you email me please?*
- *Can I call you later?*
- *I really can't discuss this now.*
- *We need to discuss this, but I can't now.*

SHARED AMENITIES

These work much better if you are on good terms.

Check your legal rights when you are considering purchasing a property with shared amenities.

Face any pitfalls before you purchase a property with shared amenities.

MORE ON JEALOUSY

Jealousy, the major cause of most neighbour problems.

When the 'victim' cannot understand why people are horrid to them in most cases the cause is jealousy. When I deal with cases of bullying, most cases are aimed at smart, attractive, successful people. I have difficulty in getting them to understand the strong emotion of jealousy, partly because it is an emotion they themselves have not experienced.

As previously mentioned here are just some causes:

- New works to a property.
- Smarter car.
- Successful career.
- Children at good schools.
- Perceived intellectual superiority.
- Popularity.
- Happiness.
- Material possessions.
- Successful personal and family relationships.
- Attractive/smart appearance.

Jealousy is so powerful that it can become an illness. Most victims of jealousy are too modest to imagine anyone would be jealous of them.

Jealousy can drive people to do unpleasant things.

If you think the behaviour towards you by your neighbours is fuelled by jealousy it is best to keep your distance, be polite but keep a distance.

JOIN A RESIDENTS' ASSOCIATION OR NEIGHBOURHOOD WATCH

You will not feel alone if you belong to a group whose aim is to maintain the neighbourhood to a high standard. Often a note from a group to a neighbour who is behaving badly will do more good than a single complaint. Also, it is safer.

If you have no such group, you could think of starting your own with another neighbour?

FLAT DWELLING

If you live in a flat you are in closer proximity with your neighbours. The most common problem is from noise, especially with conversions. Before you rent or buy, be clear on how you feel about noise. If you are sensitive to noise carefully research the noise insulation factor before renting/buying.

Flat dwelling requires tolerance and exemplary behaviour, however other people behave. Behaviour will range from:

> Those who don't care about their behaviour and how it affects others.

> to

> Those who believe their own exemplary behaviour should be adopted by all around and take it upon themselves to 'police' their block.

Both extremes can cause problems and need careful handling. If rented, go through the agents. If it is a purchased property, there may be a residents' association.

PARKING

A major cause of neighbour disputes.

- Handle situations sensitively.
- Know the parking rules.
- If someone has parked indiscriminately, be polite in asking them to move.

I once had a van parked near my drive so as I couldn't see driving in or driving out. It was not illegally parked. I left the following notice:

> *May I ask you nicely not to park here as it blocks vision exiting and entering my drive. I am concerned for a young a child or elderly person. Thank you in advance.*

The van moved.

I have found an over-polite notice often works.

However rude another motorist is, respond with politeness. It is your best tool.

ACT WITH INTEGRITY

Think before you report your neighbour for anything. Can you speak to them first, before reporting?

People often report because they are cowards about speaking to their neighbour.

Think integrity. Whatever action you take ask yourself if you are acting with integrity. Acting with integrity means doing the right thing.

KEEP A DIARY

As soon as difficult behaviour starts, record it in a diary. This will give a pattern of behaviour. It gives you something to do, rather than doing nothing and letting the stress accumulate. When you see a pattern, that is the time to decide whether or not to take the matter further. Seeing behaviour written down will give a clearer picture of facts (not assumptions). You need to react to facts not emotions or assumptions. If you have to take a matter further it will show efficiency if you have a record of facts with dates and times.

Sometimes seeing the behaviour written down can prompt a realisation of overreaction and avoid a dispute.

Diary entries, plus reliable witnesses will strengthen your case.

A WAY FORWARD

- Notice when you are over-reacting to neighbour difficulties and start a programme for your own recovery before taking action. Reduce your stress and you will find it easier to manage the situation.

- Research your options, from this book, the Internet, from a professional.

- Accept what you cannot change.

- Try to feel sorry for difficult neighbours, if they were happy they wouldn't be behaving in the way they do.

- If you have been friendly, stand back for a while. Take time out to recover, then re-establish new boundaries.

- Think before you react/respond. You don't want a dispute logged against your property.

HOW CAN WE RESOLVE THIS?

A powerful question.

Listen carefully to the answer. This helps you regain your control and puts the neighbour in the position of having to articulate exactly what they want you to do.
You then have to evaluate:

- Is it a reasonable request?

- If it is petty, remember it could be important to them. *I appreciate this is important to you but it is not my responsibility/ I don't agree to your request.*

- Are you in the wrong?

- Is it something that could be discussed over coffee?

- Avoid any type of manipulation on either side.

RE-CAP

- However rude your neighbours are when they speak to you, never retaliate in the same way.
- Never accept rudeness, if your neighbour is out for an argument, walk away.
- Never ever take neighbour behaviour personally.
- Think carefully before responding.
- Don't try to be clever or get one over on them. Revenge is never sweet. It puts you in the same category.
- Know when to seek professional advice.
- However much your neighbours anger you by their behaviour do not react. By reacting, this shows that their behaviour works.
- Never put yourself in any danger.
- Try talking to your neighbour before reporting any behaviour. Many neighbours report their neighbours to the council because they are cowards. Don't be a coward. Ask nicely, if nothing is done, then report if it is a major issue.
- Get to know your neighbours before becoming too friendly. If a boss gets too friendly with their staff, it makes creating boundaries difficult. It is the same with your neighbours.
- Always ask yourself 'what is the outcome I want?'
- Ignore the petty neighbour, however, annoying it may be.
- Accept what you cannot change.

MANAGING YOUR OWN STRESS

Unfortunately, difficult neighbours don't seem to go away and if they do another one moves into the area.

You may have a very demanding career and you don't want neighbour difficulties as soon as you come back to your home. Your home is where you de-stress and needs to be your haven. Ensure that it is.

If your neighbours are worrying you take some sort of action, just talking it over with a counsellor may be all you need to do. They will help you with a personal programme of dealing with the stress.

It makes it much easier to deal with stress if you maintain the following:

- Get enough uninterrupted sleep.
- Eat a healthy diet.
- Drink enough water to keep hydrated.
- Exercise.
- Socialise.
- Take up an absorbing interest. The brain loves learning new things.
- Forgive those who have wronged you. You don't have to tell them. Just say to yourself that you forgive them.
- Accept what you cannot change.
- Move on.

'SUNBATHING IN THE NUDE, TELL NEIGHBOURS FIRST'

Extract from an article in *The Times* Newspaper, Tuesday 3 July 2018 (full article available online: thetimes.co.uk)

'Surrey Police suggest if you want to sunbathe topless, or naked, tell the neighbours next door first. Be discreet. However, if you find your neighbour leaning out of an upstairs window or standing on the top of a step ladder, then they may well be committing an offence.'

I have no further advice to add, except

BE SURE TO WEAR PLENTY OF SUNSCREEN.

NOTES

NEIGHBOUR SELF ASSESSMENT

Are you a responsible neighbour?

(this is only a guide – use pencil and you can use it again)

1. Do you introduce yourself to new neighbours?
YES/NO/SOMETIMES

2. Do you introduce yourself when you move into a new locality?
YES/NO/SOMETIMES

3. If you share a party wall(s) with your neighbours are there any appliances which make a noise on the adjoining walls?
YES/NO/SOMETIMES

4. If you own pets, are they kept under control so as not to disturb?
YES/NO/SOMETIMES

5. Do you observe parking etiquette?
YES/NO/SOMETIMES

6. Is your rubbish dealt with efficiently, tidily and hygienically?
YES/NO/SOMETIMES

7. Do you inform your neighbours of parties/gatherings?
YES/NO/SOMETIMES

8. Do you inform neighbours of building works?
YES/NO/SOMETIMES

9. Do you restrict the time and use of noisy garden equipment?
YES/NO/SOMETIMES

10. Do your guests leave your property quietly late at night?
YES/NO/SOMETIMES

11. Is your property maintained in keeping with the locality?
YES/NO/SOMETIMES

12. Are your gardens neat and tidy?
YES/NO/SOMETIMES

13. Clear safe boundaries (fencing/hedges/walls)?
YES/NO/SOMETIMES

14. Are you friendly/helpful to your neighbours?
YES/NO/SOMETIMES

15. Would your neighbours consider you responsible?
YES/NO/SOMETIMES

16. If you are a flat dweller do you keep noise to a minimum?
YES/NO/SOMETIMES

17. Do you avoid gossip/duplicity?
YES/NO/SOMETIMES

18. Are you a nosey neighbour?
YES/NO/SOMETIMES

19. Are you able to rise above petty issues?
YES/NO/SOMETIMES

20. Are you able to forget the past and forgive neighbour behaviour?　　YES/NO/SOMETIMES

21. Do you judge your neighbours without knowing them?
YES/NO/SOMETIMES

22. Would you describe yourself as a considerate neighbour?
YES/NO/SOMETIMES

23. Respect the privacy of neighbours when they are using their garden.　　YES/NO/SOMETIMES

24. Do your prefer not to acknowledge/socialise with your neighbours?　　YES/NO/SOMETIMES

25. Are you a tolerant neighbour?
YES/NO/SOMETIMES

What did you find out about yourself from doing this questionnaire?

If you answered 'sometimes' think about it and could you make some changes?